Building
Your Best Life

Companion
Workbook

Building
Your Best Life

Companion
 *Workbook*

MERIE WEISMILLER WALLACE,
MFA, SMPSP, CBCP

ARCHWAY
PUBLISHING

Illustrations by Cassie Alisande Wallace
Cover photographs by Merie Weismiller Wallace
Author portrait photograph by Alexander Schottky

Archway Publishing books may be ordered through booksellers or by contacting:

Archway Publishing
1663 Liberty Drive
Bloomington, IN 47403
www.archwaypublishing.com
844-669-3957

The views expressed in this work are solely those of the author and do not necessarily reflect the views of the publisher, and the publisher hereby disclaims any responsibility for them.

ISBN: 978-1-6657-5538-2 (sc)
ISBN: 978-1-6657-5539-9 (e)

Print information available on the last page.

Archway Publishing rev. date: 06/12/2024

Message from the Author

This is your ❧ *Workbook*. It will end up holding important realizations and truths, and will be your guide forward as you build a meaningful life you'll love to live. Consider the material with honesty and intention, and don't get stressed about anything — take it easy and have fun with it, it's all about you!

Sometimes you'll simply be listing ideas, and other times you'll write out your reactions. It doesn't have to be perfect. It's fine to be spontaneous and quickly jot down what pops into your head, or to take your time and explore the ideas. If something seems difficult or ideas aren't coming to you, just move through areas of uncertainty with a basic, honest effort. You can always go back and add more answers if ideas come to you later, and I encourage you to do that.

Here's a tip: when you feel interest or excitement as you tell your truth, it boosts your results and opens the gates to inspiration! Sometimes looking at ourselves can be difficult, but trust me, it's worth it as you start to understand your strengths. Just do your best when you write, and always be honest, even about uncertainty; you are in a process, so you can't know everything you need to know — yet. State what you think and feel at the moment you are writing. Remember, this is *your* life. You are the captain of this remarkable ship, on your way to a life you'll love to live.

Enjoy the process!

Sincerely,
Merie Weismiller Wallace

Contents

🕊 Workbook page 1 – From Chapter 1 – MAKE IT BETTER............................ 1

🕊 Workbook page 2 – From Chapter 1 – THE HAPPY LIST....................... 2

🕊 Workbook page 3 – From Chapter 1 – YOU'RE UNIQUELY YOU.............. 3

🕊 Workbook page 4 – From Chapter 2 –
      I WOULD LIKE TO CHANGE ABOUT MYSELF LIST 4

🕊 Workbook page 5 – From Chapter 2 –
      YOUR HEALTHY AUTHENTIC SELF 5

🕊 Workbook page 6 – From Chapter 2 –
      I WOULD LIKE TO CHANGE MY LIFE LIST 6

🕊 Workbook page 7 – From Chapter 3 –
      SENTENCES THAT MAKE YOU HAPPY 7

🕊 Workbook page 8 – From Chapter 3 –
      ONE SMALL THING YOU'D LIKE TO CHANGE 8

🕊 Workbook page 9 – From Chapter 3 –
      DREAMS YOU WANT TO COME TRUE LIST................... 9

🕊 Workbook page 10 – From Chapter 3 –
      YOUR QUESTIONS / UNSURE LIST 10

🕊 Workbook page 11 – From Chapter 4 –
      THE LIFE YOU WOULD LOVE TO LIVE 11

🕊 Workbook page 12 – From Chapter 4 – THIS MATTERS! LIST 12

🕊 Workbook page 13 – From Chapter 4 –
      SYNCHRONICITY AND COINCIDENCE LIST 13

🕊 Workbook page 14 – From Chapter 5 – YOUR TALENTS LIST.................... 14

🕊 Workbook page 15 – From Chapter 5 – YOUR INTERESTS LIST 15

🕊 Workbook page 16 – From Chapter 5 – THE THINGS YOU LOVE............ 16

🕊 Workbook page 17 – From Chapter 6 – THESE MATTER SENTENCES 17

🕊 Workbook page 18 – From Chapter 6 –
         PEOPLE AND RELATIONSHIPS LIST 18

🕊 Workbook page 19 – From Chapter 6 – THE MESSES................................ 19

🕊 Workbook page 20 – From Chapter 7 – PERFECT LIFE LIST 20

🕊 Workbook page 21 – From Chapter 7 – FIX THE WORLD LIST 21

🕊 Workbook page 22 – From Chapter 7 – FUN AND RECREATION LIST... 22

🕊 Workbook page 23 – From Chapter 7 –
         YOUR FAVORITE THINGS IN LIFE NOW 23

🕊 Workbook page 24 – From Chapter 8 – YOUR OBSTACLES LIST 24

🕊 Workbook page 25 – From Chapter 8 –
         STEPS TO RESOLVE OBSTACLES LIST 25

🕊 Workbook page 26 – From Chapter 8 –
         INTERESTING JOBS & CAREERS LIST 26

🕊 Workbook page 27 – From Chapter 8 –
         TOP 5 FAVORITE JOBS OR CAREERS 27

🕊 Workbook page 28 – From Chapter 9 –
         3 LONG-TERM GOALS AND OBJECTIVES...................... 28

🕊 Workbook page 29 – From Chapter 9 –
         YOUR LONG-TERM GOALS AND OBJECTIVES............. 29

🕊 Workbook page 30 – From Chapter 9 –
         THE STEPS TO GET WHERE YOU WANT TO GO 30

❧ Workbook page 31 – From Chapter 10 – TO-DO LIST 31

❧ Workbook page 32 – From Chapter 10 –
                         POSITIVE AFFIRMATIONS FOR CHANGE 32

❧ Workbook Journaling Pages 33

Workbook page 1 – From Chapter 1
– MAKE IT BETTER

What would make your life better today:

1. _____

2. _____

3. _____

4. _____

5. _____

Now, for each, add three steps that you can take to head in that direction:

1. _____

   A. _____

   B. _____

   C. _____

2. _____

    A. _____

    B. _____

    C. _____

3. _____

    A. _____

    B. _____

    C. _____

4. _____

    A. _____

    B. _____

    C. _____

5. _____

    A. _____

    B. _____

    C. _____

❧ Workbook page 2 – From Chapter 1
– THE HAPPY LIST

In your life, what makes you happy now:

1. _____

2. _____

3. _____

4. _____

5. _____

6. _____

7. _____

8. _____

9. _____

10. _____

11. _____

12. _____

13. _____

14. _____

What do you *wish* you had, what would make you happy if it was in your life?

1. _____

2. _____

3. _____

4. _____

5. _____

6. _____

7. _____

8. _____

9. _____

10. _____

11. _____

12. _____

13. _____

14. _____

15. _____

16. _____

17. _____

18. _____

19. _____

🔑 Workbook page 3 – From Chapter 1
– YOU'RE UNIQUELY YOU

Answer these in as much detail as possible:

1. What makes you unique and different from others around you is:

   _____

   _____

2. The positive qualities you can describe about yourself are:

   _____

   _____

3. Some of your abilities, talents and skills are:

   _____

   _____

4. The things you would like to improve are:

   _____

   _____

5. The things you are most interested in are:

   _____

   _____

6. The things you think are beautiful are:

   _____

   _____

7. Your idea of funny is:

   _____

   _____

8. Whenever you see _____ you think it is so cool:

_____

_____

9. Something you saw the other day that you liked is:

_____

_____

10. All the goals you have for yourself (that you can think of right now) are:

_____

_____

11. If you had a magic wand, you would change these things in your life right now:

_____

_____

12. You feel happy when you think of these things:

_____

_____

13. If dreams came true you would:

_____

_____

14. If you didn't feel shy or embarrassed or hesitant you would gladly:

_____

_____

15. If you suddenly had a month of free time and sufficient money you would:

_____

_____

16. You love:

_____

_____

🔑 **Workbook page 4 – From Chapter 2**
– I WOULD LIKE TO CHANGE ABOUT MYSELF LIST

What do you think needs improvement about yourself? These might be deficiencies, illnesses, troubles, bad habits, or simply strengths that need polishing.

1. _____

2. _____

3. _____

4. _____

5. _____

6. _____

7. _____

8. _____

9. _____

10. _____

11. _____

12. _____

13. _____

14. _____

15. _____

16. _____

17. _____

18. _____

19. _____

20. _____

21. _____

22. _____

23. _____

24. _____

25. _____

26. _____

27. _____

28. _____

29. _____

30. _____

31. _____

❧ Workbook page 5 – From Chapter 2
– YOUR HEALTHY AUTHENTIC SELF

What is your vision of your healthy, true inner self? Include what you like about yourself now, your good traits, and who you feel yourself to be deep down. Maybe some are who you were as a child that you'd like to get back to. What seems genuinely, uniquely you?

1. _____

2. _____

3. _____

4. _____

5. _____

6. _____

7. _____

8. _____

9. _____

10. _____

11. _____

12. _____

13. _____

14. _____

15. _____

16. _____

17. _____

18. _____

19. _____

20. _____

21. _____

22. _____

23. _____

24. _____

25. _____

26. _____

27. _____

28. _____

29. _____

30. _____

31. _____

🔑 Workbook page 6 – From Chapter 2
– I WOULD LIKE TO CHANGE MY LIFE LIST

List three or more important things that you would like to change in your life right now. Is something missing? Is something happening that you don't like? Does anything feel like it's going wrong? These can be anything from small needed corrections to big life changes!

What would you like to fix?   **In this column write something good about the point on the left**

1. _____   _____

2. _____   _____

3. _____   _____

4. _____   _____

5. _____   _____

6. _____   _____

7. _____   _____

8. _____   _____

9. _____   _____

10. _____   _____

11. _____   _____

12. _____   _____

13. _____   _____

14. _____   _____

15. _____   _____

16. _____   _____

17. _____   _____

18. _____   _____

19. _____   _____

20. _____   _____

21. _____   _____

22. _____   _____

23. _____   _____

24. _____   _____

25. _____   _____

26. _____   _____

27. _____   _____

28. _____   _____

🔑 Workbook page 7 – From Chapter 3
– SENTENCES THAT MAKE YOU HAPPY

For each of the things you listed on the left column of 🔑Workbook page 6, write a statement, in the present, as if it had already changed to the way you want it.

For example, "I eat too much junk food " becomes "I stopped eating junk food, and I'm feeling so much better." "I'm so glad that things are going well with _____." "Now that I'm _____, I'm enjoying my _____ so much more." "I feel great now that I can _____."

1. _____

2. _____

3. _____

4. _____

5. _____

6. _____

7. _____

8. _____

9. _____

10. _____

11. _____

12. _____

13. _____

14. _____

15. _____

16. _____

17. _____

18. _____

19. _____

20. _____

21. _____

22. _____

23. _____

24. _____

25. _____

Now, reread those sentences. Take the time to imagine clearly that each of these positive statements is true. Feel how nice it is that each thing is now how you want it to be! Put a check next to the ones you feel strongest about!

❧ Workbook page 8 – From Chapter 3 – ONE SMALL THING YOU'D LIKE TO CHANGE

1. For fun, try adding another small thing that you want to change. Make sure you don't have it now, but that you want it. Make sure this a doable, small thing, not an enormous change.

_____

_____

_____

_____

2. Next, write out a statement as if that small thing is already done and completed, and also how you feel great about the new way it is. Like "I feel great now that I have _____!"

_____

_____

_____

_____

3. Imagine and visualize details of that, and enjoy how they feel, look, taste. Who is there with you in your success? What tools, equipment or beautiful things are part of it? Use imagination!

_____

_____

_____

_____

4. Write down one or more obvious action steps you can take and then act on it. You might find a jar and label it and put some cash into it every day, make a call to ask about how to get started, make a call to get a little side work to help pay for it, throw things away that are not compatible with it, and so on. These are just examples. Use your creative mind and heart to come up with something similar that applies to your small goal and situation.

A. _____

B. _____

C. _____

D. _____

E. _____

5. Reread and feel the small goal statement on this ❧Workbook page 8 #1 at least once every day, until it has come true, until it has shifted and you like it now, or its equivalent has happened and you don't need to keep working toward it anymore.

6. Take actions steps toward it, small or large, daily. It will happen!

1. Write out four things, big or small, that you would love to have in your future, or to fill your life now with. These are dreams you'd love to have come true about recreation, work, school, family, friends, adventure, etc.:

    A. _____

    B. _____

    C. _____

    D. _____

2. Now, write out a statement for each as if it is already true and you feel great about it!

    E. _____

    F. _____

    G. _____

    H. _____

3. Imagine and visualize details of those items and enjoy each aspect. Who is there with you? What tools, equipment, or beautiful things are part of it?

_____

_____

_____

_____

_____

4. Then for items A – D, above, write down one or more obvious steps you can take. For example, you could open a bank account, make a call, get an application, clean up to make room. Use your creative mind and heart to come up with steps that apply to your A – D goals.

_____

_____

_____

_____

_____

Reread, and feel, the statements in #2, above, at least once every day, until each has come true or its equivalent has happened and you don't need to keep working toward it anymore. Take action steps toward them, small or large, daily.

❧ Workbook page 10 – From Chapter 3
– YOUR QUESTIONS / UNSURE LIST

What specific areas in your future life are you unsure of?

Write out four examples, big or small, that you can think of in response to each of these tasks:

1. In which important areas of life – work, school, people, adventure, etc. – do you honestly feel you don't know how to choose what would work best for you in your future life?

   A. _____

   B. _____

   C. _____

   D. _____

2. Write out a statement about each area as if you already know what you want and you feel great about it: "I know what I care about and love to do when it comes to _____ (work, school, people, adventure etc.), and I can't wait to get started!" Imagine, visualize, and write down details, enjoy each thing as you write it, use imagination and stretch yourself a bit:

   E. _____

   F. _____

G. _____

H. _____

3. Now, write down one or more obvious steps you can take to get from A – D to E – H. Use imagination to come up with steps that apply specifically.

_____

_____

_____

_____

_____

_____

_____

_____

_____

_____

Reread, feel, and take steps toward the statements in #2, above, at least once every day until each of them has come true, its equivalent has happened as life presented, or you have changed your goal and are pursuing something else this way instead.

Take active steps from #3, above toward achieving these dreams, hopes, and intentions, small or large, daily.

❧ Workbook page 11 – From Chapter 4
– THE LIFE YOU WOULD LOVE TO LIVE

Rewrite the positive statements from ❧Workbook pages 7 – 10. From ❧Workbook page 7, pick the top 10 statements that make you feel energized and rewrite them in full, direct sentences here:

From ❧Workbook page 7:

1. _____

2. _____

3. _____

4. _____

5. _____

6. _____

7. _____

8. _____

9. _____

10. _____

From ❦Workbook page 8 #2:

_____

_____

_____

_____

_____

_____

From ❦Workbook page 9 #2:

E. _____

F. _____

G. _____

H. _____

From ❦Workbook page 10 #2:

E. _____

F. _____

G. _____

H. _____

Workbook page 12 – From Chapter 4 – THIS MATTERS! LIST

This page is active; every time you think of something that you like, care about, are grateful for, or that matter to you, big or small, write it here! These might be things that you think are cool, or that made you happy recently, or are part of your positive statements list from Workbook pages 7 and 11.

Write 20 things that matter:

1. _____

_____

2. _____

_____

3. _____

_____

4. _____

_____

5. _____

_____

6. _____

_____

7. _____

_____

8. _____

9. _____

10. _____

11. _____

12. _____

13. _____

14. _____

15. _____

16. _____

17. _____

18. _____

19. _____

20. _____

❧ Workbook page 13 – From Chapter 4
– SYNCHRONICITY AND COINCIDENCE LIST

Re-read the definitions of coincidence and synchronicity in Chapter 4 What Really Matters, under *"Providence Is Moving."*

Unexpected and unusual coincidences occur, each time they do, write them here. This page is active, every time something synchronous happens, big or small, write it here. When you do, you will start to notice them happening more often, and how they serve you.

1. _____

_____

2. _____

_____

3. _____

_____

4. _____

_____

5. _____

_____

6. _____

_____

7. _____

_____

8. _____

_____

9. _____

_____

10. _____

_____

11. _____

_____

12. _____

_____

13. _____

_____

14. _____

_____

15. _____

_____

16. _____

_____

17. _____

_____

18. _____

_____

19. _____

_____

20. _____

_____

🕭 Workbook page 14 – From Chapter 5 – YOUR TALENTS LIST

Envision and feel the feelings of how good it would feel if you could use your talents on a large scale for good pay while helping large numbers of people or nature. If you are not sure what jobs match your talents, you can leave that part blank for now – and make a note on 🕭Workbook page 26 to research careers requiring that talent.

Talents	**How can those talents be used to help people?**
1. _____	_____
2. _____	_____
3. _____	_____
4. _____	_____
5. _____	_____
6. _____	_____
7. _____	_____
8. _____	_____
9. _____	_____

10. _____ _____

11. _____ _____

12. _____ _____

13. _____ _____

14. _____ _____

15. _____ _____

16. _____ _____

17. _____ _____

18. _____ _____

19. _____ _____

20. _____ _____

21. _____ _____

22. _____ _____

23. _____ _____

24. _____ _____

25. _____ _____

26. _____ _____

Now, add your **Talents** from this page to your **This Matters!** list on ✎Workbook page 12

🙌 **Workbook page 15 – From Chapter 5**
– YOUR INTERESTS LIST

List the things that interest you, including uncommon interests that you'd like to do with other people, cool things you would actually want to do. Imagine yourself enjoying doing these things, alone or with others, or sharing your successes with people who care about you. Anything creative, interesting, fun!

1. _____

_____

2. _____

_____

3. _____

_____

4. _____

_____

5. _____

_____

6. _____

_____

7. _____

_____

8. _____

_____

9. _____

_____

10. _____

_____

11. _____

_____

12. _____

_____

13. _____

_____

14. _____

_____

15. _____

_____

16. _____

_____

17. _____

_____

18. _____

_____

19. _____

_____

20. _____

_____

Now, add your **Interests** from this page to your **This Matters!** list on Workbook page 12.

❧ Workbook page 16 – From Chapter 5 – THE THINGS YOU LOVE

Write down the names of people, places, and things that you love. Take the time to *feel* your love for each thing as you write it. This is an important list, and you'll refer back to it, so take the time to name as many things as you can think of: people, food, places, fun activities, beautiful aspects of nature, animals, etc. In days to come, you'll keep adding to this list when you think of or experience anything else that you love.

1. _____

_____

2. _____

_____

3. _____

_____

4. _____

_____

5. _____

_____

6. _____

_____

7. _____

_____

8. _____

_____

9. _____

_____

10. _____

_____

11. _____

_____

12. _____

_____

13. _____

_____

14. _____

_____

15. _____

_____

16. _____

_____

17. _____

_____

18. _____

_____

19. _____

_____

20. _____

_____

When you are done, go to your **Happy List** on ❧Workbook page 2 and see if there is anything there that you want to add to this list!

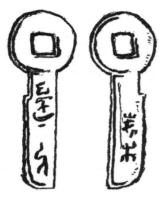

❧ Workbook page 17 – From Chapter 6 – THESE MATTER SENTENCES

Write positive statements in the present about each of things on your ❧Workbook page 12 = your **This Matters! LIST**. For example, "I love _____ and I have set it into my calendar with great plans to do it often!" "_____ matters to me, I make calls every week to support that."

1. _____

_____

2. _____

_____

3. _____

_____

4. _____

_____

5. _____

_____

6. _____

_____

7. _____

_____

8. _____

_____

9. _____

_____

10. _____

_____

11. _____

_____

12. _____

_____

13. _____

_____

14. _____

_____

15. _____

_____

16. _____

_____

17. _____

_____

18. _____

_____

19. _____

_____

20. _____

_____

Workbook page 18 – From Chapter 6 – PEOPLE AND RELATIONSHIPS LIST

List the main people in your life, for better and for worse.

1. _____
_____

2. _____
_____

3. _____
_____

4. _____
_____

5. _____
_____

6. _____
_____

7. _____
_____

8. _____
_____

9. _____

10. _____

_____

11. _____

_____

12. _____

_____

13. _____

_____

14. _____

_____

15. _____

_____

16. _____

_____

17. _____

_____

18. _____

_____

19. _____

_____

20. _____

_____

Now, put a check mark next to the names of people with whom the relationship needs improving, or less contact, and write down why. Put a star next to the ones you are happiest about, and write down why on your Happy List ❧Workbook page 2.

❧ Workbook page 19 – From Chapter 6 – THE MESSES

List the messes in your life today, and in the opposite column, what it would take to make them right.

The Messes	**What would it take to make it right for _you_?**
• Family _____	_____
_____	_____
_____	_____
• Friends and social interactions _____	_____
_____	_____
_____	_____
• Creative projects or hobbies _____	_____
_____	_____
_____	_____

- Intellectual interests _____ _____

_____ _____

_____ _____

- Employment _____ _____

_____ _____

_____ _____

- Financial overview _____ _____

_____ _____

_____ _____

- Contribution _____ _____

_____ _____

_____ _____

- Recreation _____ _____

_____ _____

_____ _____

- Health _____ _____

_____ _____

_____ _____

Look back at ❧Workbook page 4 and add more to this page if any other messes come to mind.

❧ Workbook page 20 – From Chapter 7 – PERFECT LIFE LIST

With eyes closed, *imagine* where you would like to be in 5-10 years from now. Visualize your perfect life in all its details including your perfect home, that you are financially stable, which family and friends are present, what you do for fun, what ways you are helping, etc.

Your perfect life includes:

_____

_____

_____

_____

_____

_____

_____

_____

_____

_____

⚜ Workbook page 21– From Chapter 7
– FIX THE WORLD LIST

What would you fix if you could make the world a better place? Start with your neighborhood, expand to your town, your state, your country, the whole world.

1. _____

2. _____

3. _____

4. _____

5. _____

6. _____

7. _____

8. _____

9. _____

10. _____

11. _____

12. _____

13. _____

14. _____

15. _____

16. _____

17. _____

18. _____

19. _____

20. _____

21. _____

22. _____

23. _____

24. _____

25. _____

26. _____

27. _____

28. _____

29. _____

30. _____

31. _____

32. _____

❧ Workbook page 22 – From Chapter 7
– FUN AND RECREATION LIST

What do you like to do, and love to do? What would you love to *learn* how to do?

1. _____

2. _____

3. _____

4. _____

5. _____

6. _____

7. _____

8. _____

9. _____

10. _____

11. _____

12. _____

13. _____

14. _____

15. _____

16. _____

17. _____

18. _____

19. _____

20. _____

21. _____

22. _____

23. _____

24. _____

25. _____

26. _____

27. _____

28. _____

29. _____

30. _____

31. _____

32. _____

33. _____

34. _____

❧ Workbook page 23 – From Chapter 7
– YOUR FAVORITE THINGS IN LIFE NOW

List the things you love about your life today. Write these off the top of your head now, and *then* go back to your LOVE List on ❧Workbook page 16 for more ideas. Consider all areas of your life. There will be overlap in some of these categories; in those cases, write the thing twice.

- Family _____

_____

_____

- Friends and social interactions _____

_____

_____

- Creative projects or hobbies _____

_____

_____

- Intellectual interests _____

_____

_____

- Employment _____

_____

_____

- Financial overview _____

_____

_____

- Contribution _____

_____

_____

- Recreation _____

_____

_____

- Health _____

_____

_____

❧ Workbook page 24 – From Chapter 8 – YOUR OBSTACLES LIST

Write down all the obstacles, people and situations, that you can think of that are blocking you in each of the areas of your life:

- Family _____

_____

_____

- Friends and social interactions _____

_____

_____

- Creative projects or hobbies _____

_____

_____

- Intellectual interests _____

_____

_____

- Employment _____

_____

_____

- Financial overview _____

_____

_____

- Contribution _____

_____

_____

- Recreation _____

_____

_____

- Health _____

_____

_____

- Personal Problems _____

_____

_____

- Fears _____

_____

_____

Workbook page 25 – From Chapter 8
– STEPS TO RESOLVE OBSTACLES LIST

Using your list on ❧Workbook page 24, write down some initial steps you can take to resolve each obstacle, problem or fear. For example, if an obstacle is family fighting, you might write "If I practice speaking my truth kindly, it would help my family get along."

- Family _____

_____

_____

- Friends and social interactions _____

_____

_____

- Creative projects or hobbies _____

_____

_____

- Intellectual interests _____

_____

_____

Building Your Best Life Companion Workbook

- Employment _____

_____

_____

- Financial overview _____

_____

_____

- Contribution _____

_____

_____

- Recreation _____

_____

_____

- Health _____

_____

_____

- Personal Problems _____

_____

_____

- Fears _____

_____

_____

❧ Workbook page 26 – From Chapter 8
– INTERESTING JOBS & CAREERS LIST

Make a list of the jobs and careers that excite or interest you when you imagine yourself doing well at them. (Look back at ❧Workbook page 14 your **TALENTS** for ideas)

1. _____

2. _____

3. _____

4. _____

5. _____

6. _____

7. _____

8. _____

9. _____

10. _____

11. _____

12. _____

13. _____

14. _____

15. _____

16. _____

17. _____

18. _____

19. _____

20. _____

21. _____

22. _____

23. _____

24. _____

25. _____

26. _____

27. _____

28. _____

29. _____

30. _____

31. _____

32. _____

33. _____

34. _____

❧ Workbook page 27 – From Chapter 8
– TOP 5 FAVORITE JOBS OR CAREERS

Make a list of your five favorite jobs from ❧Workbook page 26. What are your next steps, starting where you are now, to get there? Write as many steps as come to mind.

FAVORITE CAREERS	OBVIOUS STEPS TO ACHIEVE THIS
1. _____	• _____
	• _____
	• _____
2. _____	• _____
	• _____
	• _____
3. _____	• _____
	• _____
	• _____
4. _____	• _____
	• _____
	• _____

5. _____

           • _____

           • _____

           • _____

6. _____

           • _____

           • _____

           • _____

7. _____

           • _____

           • _____

           • _____

8. _____

           • _____

           • _____

           • _____

9. _____

           • _____

           • _____

           • _____

10. _____

           • _____

           • _____

           • _____

❧ Workbook page 28 – From Chapter 9
– 3 LONG-TERM GOALS AND OBJECTIVES

Choosing from the areas of your life: Family, Friends & Social Interactions, Creative projects & hobbies, Intellectual interests, Employment, Financial overview, Contribution, Recreation, & Health:

1. Write down **three** important long-term goals and objectives, make sure each is from a different area of your life.

    A. _____

    B. _____

    C. _____

2. Write a full sentence about each of those three long-term goals as if they are already true in the present. Assign a date to your goals if you can, and write out a detailed description.

    A. _____

    B. _____

    C. _____

3. Take the time now to reread and feel great about each one of those three! Feel belief that it is already true and possible, just a matter of time, as sure and straightforward as "I intend to walk to the next room." Visualize them and imagine yourself happy in each of the three visualizations. What does each of these situations look like physically?

Who else is there? Know that it is part of you, you have it, and it exists in the unseen. Envision and visualize yourself there, receiving exactly what you want and need.

4. How would you *feel* if you had achieved your goals? *Read and feel* the happiness and excitement of each! *Feel grateful* that you get to live your dreams!

5. Write down as many steps as you can think of to go forward from where you are now, today, for each of these goals. This is a living document, check things off as you complete them. Save the lists to see how far you've come!

A. _____

B. _____

C. _____

D. _____

E. _____

F. _____

G. _____

H. _____

I. _____

J. _____

K. _____

Going forward, write down and follow through on every **Inspired Idea** you have! When you are coming from your vision, when you are authentic, what you are attracted to is on your path. Like attracts like. You can start where you are today – starting with this ✺Workbook – holding your authentic goals in mind, you are taking the first steps.

❧ Workbook page 29 – From Chapter 9
– YOUR LONG-TERM GOALS AND OBJECTIVES

The areas of your life: Family, Friends & Social Interactions, Creative projects & hobbies, Intellectual interests, Employment, Financial overview, Contribution, Recreation, & Health

Write down at least one important long-term goal and objective for each of the remaining parts of your life. Write out each goal as a sentence in the present tense. Believe it, *feel* knowing it's what you're going to do. Feel *sure* that it is going to happen – that or something different and good. Visualize and imagine it in detail, colors, people, places; see yourself happy in it. Feel the happiness and excitement of each goal! Feel actual gratitude that you get to live your dreams! Keep these lists alive by adding more good ideas as they come to mind.

1. Write down at least one important long-term goal and objective for each of the remaining parts of your life.

    A. _____

    B. _____

    C. _____

    D. _____

    E. _____

    F. _____

2. Write a full sentence about each of your six long-term goals as if they are already true in the present. Assign a date to your goals, and write out a detailed description.

A. _____

B. _____

C. _____

D. _____

E. _____

F. _____

Take the time now to reread and feel great about each one of those three. Feel belief that it is already true and possible, it is just a matter of time. -What does each of these situations look like physically? Who else is there? Know that it is part of you, you have it, and it exists in the unseen. Envision and visualize yourself there, receiving exactly what you want and need.

3. How will you *feel* when you have achieved your goals? *Read and feel* the happiness and excitement of each! *Feel grateful* that you get to live your dreams!

4. Write down as many steps as you can think of to go forward from where you are now, today, for each of these goals. This is a living document, check things off as you complete them. Save the lists to see how far you've come!

A. _____

B. _____

C. _____

D. _____

E. _____

F. _____

Review ✍Workbook pages 20 and 23 for what your perfect life looks like. What goals have you written there? Update and revise those pages, or add from them to this page if needed.

✿ Workbook page 30 – From Chapter 9
– THE STEPS TO GET WHERE YOU WANT TO GO

Choosing from the areas of your life: Family, Friends & Social Interactions, Creative projects & hobbies, Intellectual interests, Employment, Financial overview, Contribution, Recreation, & Health:

Using your lists on ✿Workbook page 28 #5 and 29 #4, write down as many steps, large and small, as you can think of now that are necessary to get from where you are today to fulfilling each of the long-term goals. This is a living document, check things off as you complete them. Save the lists to see how far you've come!

• Steps toward Family Goals

_____

_____

• Steps toward Friends and social interactions Goals

_____

_____

• Steps toward Creative projects or hobbies Goals

_____

_____

- Steps toward Intellectual interests Goals

_____

_____

- Steps toward Employment Goals

_____

_____

- Steps toward Financial overview Goals

_____

_____

- Steps toward Contribution Goals

_____

_____

- Steps toward Recreation Goals

_____

_____

- Steps toward Health Goals

_____

_____

_____

◆ Workbook page 31 – From Chapter 10 – TO-DO LIST

Hold your vision for each area of your life and create your to-do list with next indicated action steps accordingly:

- Family

_____

_____

- Friends and social interactions

_____

_____

- Creative projects or hobbies

_____

_____

- Intellectual interests

_____

_____

- Employment

_____

_____

_____

- Financial overview

_____

_____

_____

- Contribution

_____

_____

_____

- Recreation

_____

_____

_____

- Health

_____

_____

_____

❧ Workbook page 32 – From Chapter 10
– POSITIVE AFFIRMATIONS
FOR CHANGE

Carefully write positive affirmations for the changes that you want to bring in to you life. Reread the book Chapter 10 section on affirmations if you need to.

1. _____

_____

_____

2. _____

_____

_____

3. _____

_____

_____

4. _____

_____

_____

5. _____

_____

_____

6. _____

_____

_____

7. _____

_____

_____

8. _____

_____

_____

9. _____

_____

_____

10. _____

_____

_____

Workbook Journaling Pages

Printed in the United States
by Baker & Taylor Publisher Services